SKUNKS!

A MY INCREDIBLE WORLD PICTURE BOOK

MY INCREDIBLE WORLD

Skunks live all over North and South America.

Skunks have long claws.
Perfect for digging up food!

A skunk's paw has five toes.
Just like a person!

Skunks cannot see more than 10 feet in front of them.

Skunks often sleep in leaf-lined dens.

Skunks have excellent senses of smell and hearing.

Mother skunks usually have 4-6 babies in a litter.

Baby skunks are called kits.
Aren't they cute?

Skunks live in woodland areas, near farms and even in cities!

Skunk fur can be black-and-white, brown and even cream or ginger-colored.

Skunks dig holes in dirt and lawns in search of grubs and worms.

All skunks have stripes,
except for albino skunks.

Most skunks live 2 to 3 years.

Skunks can run up to
5 miles an hour.

Skunks gather in communal dens for warmth.

A skunk's worst enemies are coyotes, bobcats and owls.

Some people have pet skunks!

Skunks can produce a strong
smell to warn potential predators.

Skunks have glands in their bottoms that spray stinky liquid up to 12 feet!

Skunks can weigh up to
18 pounds!

Skunks are nocturnal, meaning they sleep during the day and look for food at night.

Skunks are smart!

Made in the USA
Middletown, DE
05 March 2020